First Published in the UK by VPAH imprint via Kindle Direct Publishing, 2021

Text Copyright © 2021 Pamela Nyatanga

Illustrations Copyright © 2021 Jake Biggin

The moral rights of the author and illustrator has been asserted.

All rights reserved.

No part of this book may be used or reproduced in any manner whatsoever without written permission except in the case of brief quotations embodied in critical articles and reviews.

ISBN: 978-1-3999-0777-4

A CIP catalogue record for this book is available from the British Library

Dedication:

P.N: For Luisa. He will always be with you. x

J.B: Remembering Jemima, Olive, James & Lawrence
(and for S & A of course xx)

When Grandad Visited This World

Written by Pamela Nyatanga

Illustrated by Jake Biggin

Grandad loved to read.

He would read newspapers, story books, road signs, letters and maps - often he read maps to find directions after he had gotten lost!

He once told me about a poem he had read that made him
remember what the explanation for his life was.
The paragraph was by Etienne de Grellet (a clever person)
and it reads like this:

"I shall pass this way but once.

Any good, therefore,

that I can do

or any kindness that I can show to any human being,

Let me do it now.

Let me not defer nor neglect it,

For I shall not pass this way again"

I think grandad liked these words because they made him remember to always be kind to others and to always treat others with love.

When my grandad was born, the world was excited to have such an awesome visitor. The sun shone so brightly: one could only look at it with sunglasses. The stars twinkled like super diamonds in the sky.

The sky was a dazzling blue, reflecting the amazing ocean colours.

And well, the moon did shine as bright as day.

To sum it up, it was a great day, and grandad was full of life.

His body carried his life.

My grandad's body was medium built, topped with a head of grey-black hairs, big ears, brown eyes, a big smile and a big heart.

Life means breathing and living.
It is one of the miracles of the world.

I call it a miracle because I don't think anyone can simply
explain what life is.

Life is a journey – it starts and ends somewhere.

Grandad once told me that the journey of life is there for us to make the most of.
We make the most of life by being caring to ourselves and to others, and also by enjoying the things we love doing.

Because his body was full of life, he was always around us: his family and friends.

We had the best time!

Sometimes he would tell me ridiculously funny stories, which would make us laugh and laugh, at times until tears of joy ran down our cheeks!

I also made him laugh a lot with my funny stories too - Hahaha!

Grandad thought about other people's feelings.

He saw the beauty in people and everything around him.

He listened carefully and cared very much about others, especially me.

At other times, he would visit my school or pick me up after school.
I would feel so proud walking hand in hand with him.

I loved our walks, because I could always talk to him and he was a good listener.

Those big ears helped! He even found my stories about unicorns and super-heroes racing around space fascinating.

Even though he could not run as fast as me, he would always encourage me to race with him.

I always won of course!

He would sometimes buy me treats like ice-cream, which my parents thought was naughty.

But he was 'good-naughty', which only grandads can be! He also showed me incredibly good manners, like saying 'thank you' when someone gives me way and 'please' when I am asking for something. I learnt a lot of good things from him.

Oh! And he gave the best cuddles - they were so warm and comforting.

One day, as he became very sick, he was reminded that his journey in the world would soon be over.
It seemed so soon because he was still having fun with everyone.
He felt he still had a lot to do, but his body felt a bit weaker and unwell, which meant we could not really continue to have fun in the same way as before.

Nobody could really tell or predict when the actual day of him leaving the world would be, which made everything cloudy, dark, uncomfortable and difficult.

He was no longer able to do the things that he loved doing.
Sometimes he could not remember me or talk to me. But, in that dark cloud was a silver lining: he had done all the good things that he could do including having made me, my family and a lot of other people incredibly happy.

Following this, he was only with us for a short time longer, then one day, his breath and then, therefore his life left his body.

This is when he died.

When life ends, people call that death. I think his breath and his life returned to the universe – up with the stars, sun, moon, and sky.

Some people refer to his breath and life as his spirit or his soul.

When someone dies, people often say that they are "no longer with us" or "they have passed away".

And, because it is not possible to keep their bodies with us forever, we hold a special event called a funeral, then ask the Earth to look after it in a special place called a grave.

I also discovered that some adults do not really want to talk about dying as they think it is an awfully bad thing - they feel that it is unfair that they no longer have grandad around.

When someone dies, I think some people are shocked and some are not ready for that person to leave this world and maybe others, because they are scared about what might happen in the future, want to control a lot, even those things out of their control.

What I realised was that everyone's feelings are important.

I still miss seeing him, talking to him. And cuddling him.

In time, people dealt with the absence of grandad better.

They realised that just because he was dead did not mean that he could no longer be a part of us; I always remember grandad and so does everyone else.

Sometimes we remember him quietly in our minds, and other times we speak up about him.

Although I cannot feel his cuddles, nor hear his voice, nor see him, I always carry his memory in my heart and mind.

Some people describe this remembrance as etching because no matter what, no-one can ever remove his memory from me.

I remember grandad.

I REMEMBER him vividly.

I remember him when I look at the sky.

I remember him when I see the sun, moon, and stars.

I even think he is one of the stars twinkling and winking at me from high above.

When it rains, I think it sounds as though the universe is applauding and telling me what a great job grandad did during his visit to this world. I realise I was so lucky to have had him as my amazing grandad.

I remember grandad when I go for walks.
The trees remind me of him: old and wise, beautiful, bold, standing proud and also, how important he was to mine and others' lives.

I remember him when I look at photographs of us.
I have found it much easier to talk to my friends and to share stories about our grandads- alive or dead. I love talking about how wonderful he was and the fun things we did together.

I still do feel sad knowing I will never see him in person again, but I know I can talk to others about my feelings and it helps me feel better inside.

I sometimes write letters to him, telling him what I have been up to- those superheroes have a new space-mission!

One day when I am older, I will write a book about grandad and me or even a very jolly song.

Although he was a visitor to this world, I know that I will always carry grandad in my heart.

I will always remember him.

The End

Thank you:
Brian and Priscilla, for encouraging me to never shy away from uncomfortable emotions.
Aanand, for being my first audience and for your fun, active mind.
Hrithik, for making me realise I can do it, if I just think it.
Vivek, for quietly holding my hand all the time.
Beth, for always having your glass (and mine) more than half full.
And to my grandparents - for taking the fear out of impermanence and for loving us.

Printed in Great Britain
by Amazon